WINE LORE

BY THE SAME AUTHOR

The Complete Book of Drink

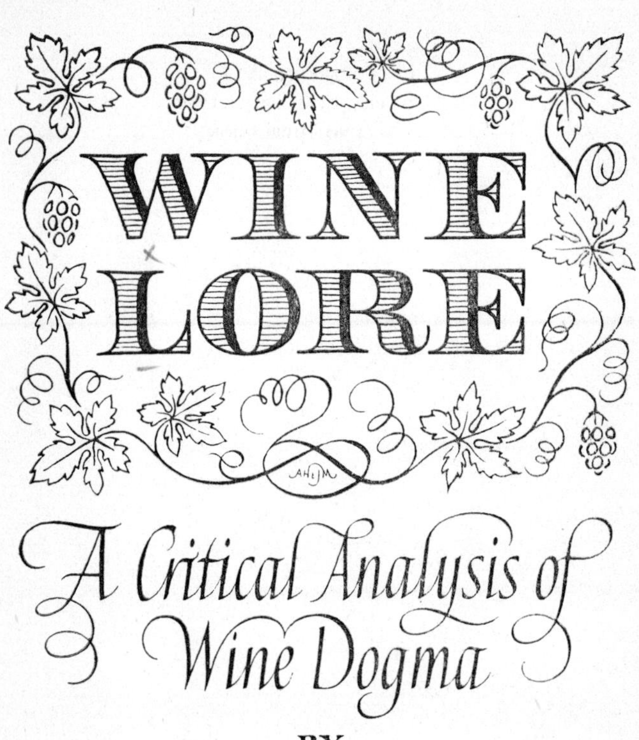

BY

T·E·CARLING

Author of the "Complete Book of Drink"

Practical Press Ltd

SECOND IMPRESSION

PRINTED IN GREAT BRITAIN
BY C. J. FARNCOMBE AND SONS LTD.,
CROYDON, SURREY

FOREWORD

THE writer of this volume has no quarrel with the connoisseurs, still less does he wish to cross swords with the Philistines. There is generally a happy medium between extremes, which is the path the average person usually prefers to take, and this book is written for the benefit of those who have no fixed ideas concerning wine, and wish to be allowed to enjoy it their own way, but who, nevertheless, may desire to take advantage of advice, from whatever quarter it may come.

No attempt is made here to lay down any fresh dogma, the purpose being rather to make a critical examination of the truths, and also the half-truths, which have emanated from connoisseurs and would-be connoisseurs from time to time in the past, so that the reader may be at liberty to judge for himself the merits of such opinions, and form his own conclusions.

The writer is a lover of wine, whether it be of humble and lowly origin, or a masterpiece of painstaking skill and craftsmanship. Both have their place in the order of things. Both are the result of hard work, patience, and an endeavour to give of the best, whether that best be, let us say, a simple melody, or a complicated harmony. If the one may be likened to a fugue, a masterpiece of interwoven subtleties that only a trained taste can fully appreciate, the other may be compared to a plain, ordinary song, appealing to all alike. A surfeit of fugues is, however, likely to pall, and it is then that the unpretentious melody pleases most.

With wine, one must first of all learn to appreciate the simple melody before aspiring to the mighty fugue, and even after thus graduating, refresh the taste by returning from time to time to the plain and ordinary.

Our musical analogy can be carried a step further: the presentation of a fugue, unless rendered in accordance with the composer's intentions, may make the whole work completely unacceptable. Equally so, the serving of a fine vintage wine, unless correctly carried out, may quite annul all the work of the craftsman who produced it.

There is, therefore, much to be said in favour of following certain rules in the drinking of wine, especially when those rules are the result of years of experience on the part of others.

CONTENTS

1

NOTES ON VINIFICATION

THERE is still much ignorance concerning wine, in spite of the spate of literature on the subject which has been disseminated from time immemorial. The truth is that wine is a very subtle commodity, and is produced in such vast quantities and diverse qualities that it is a matter of a life-time's study to comprehend and appreciate fully the many facets that the subject presents. It is natural, therefore, that a certain amount of divergence of opinion should exist, especially as individual tastes are bound to differ.

In order to judge correctly the value of any arguments on this subject, it is necessary to know the broad principles of vinification, and these, therefore, are briefly recounted below.

Wine can be divided into three main categories:

1 *Natural* (to which no addition has been made)

This group embraces the still, beverage wines, which are light in alcohol, because fermentation ceases after a certain degree of spirit has been produced. These wines will be either dry, medium dry, or sweet, according to the sugar content of the grape employed. In the case of a grape with a low sugar content, the whole of this will be converted before the degree of alcoholic saturation which checks the fermentation is reached, thus producing a completely dry wine.

2 *Fortified* (to which spirit has been added)

This group includes wines usually described as dessert wines. They are mainly sweet to a degree, because the spirit is added at an early stage, thus checking the fermentation, and leaving a large proportion of unconverted grape sugar; but *dry* fortified wines, such as Fino Sherry, are also produced. These wines will be high in alcoholic strength owing to the added spirit, which is usually grape spirit (brandy), though in the case of Madeira, cane spirit is used.

3 *Made* (to which a liqueur has been added)

This group comprises the sparkling wines, which usually have a dosage of a liqueur of sugar dissolved in old wine, to ensure that a sufficiency of gas is produced during the seondary fermentation, which takes place in the bottle.

The natural colour of wine is either red, rosé or white. The first is made from black grapes, but white wines can be made from either white or black grapes. In the latter case the result is achieved by excluding the skins, which contain the pigment, from the fermenting grape juice (" must "). White wines are not truly white, but range from pale amber to dark golden.

Rosé wines are produced by removal from the " must " of the black skins shortly after fermentation has commenced. These are the true rosé wines. Other rosé wines are made by mixing black and white grapes for fermenting together, or by blending red and white wine, whilst others may be faked by the addition of cochineal to white wine.

All wines can be divided according to whether they are blended or unblended, the latter being made from the grapes of one vineyard of one particular year. The blending of wines is carried out in order to produce a wine complete in itself, by " marrying " together similar wines, some of which may be lacking in certain qualities such as body, colour, etc., so that the different qualities of each will augment the qualities of the whole. Wines are also blended to produce and maintain a standard.

Again wines can be subdivided according to whether they have matured in wood or in bottle. The latter usually have first to spend some time in cask, generally about two years.

The vinification is carried out broadly in the following manner, although each type of wine has its modifications:

The grapes are picked, and then pressed almost immediately. The fresh grape juice at once commences to froth and bubble, owing to the production of carbonic acid gas from the conversion of the sugar into alcohol. The fermentation is initiated by the bloom on the outside of the grape,

which is actually a form of yeast. After the first fermentation has ceased, all solid matter sinks to the bottom of the cask or vat holding the wine, and this wine is then racked—that is, drawn off from its lees into fresh casks. Later a secondary fermentation takes place, and after a second racking, or more, the wine is allowed to mature in wood, usually from two to three years, before being bottled.

With sparkling wines, the secondary fermentation is allowed to take place in the bottle, thus retaining the gas, which gives these wines their sparkling character.

Most wines go on maturing in bottle, and in the process throw a deposit, the disturbance of which will foul the wine.

For this reason, wines old in bottle have to be carefully decanted before use, or most carefully poured from the bottle.

In the case of sparkling wines, the deposit must be removed before the wine is shipped, otherwise, owing to the presence of the gas, the wine would be fouled immediately upon drawing the cork. This removal of the deposit is done by a process of *dégorgement* which consists of first bringing down the deposit on to the cork by storing the bottles at an almost vertical angle. When the deposit has settled on the cork, the neck of the bottle is frozen, the cork is then drawn, and the pellet of ice is expelled by reason of the pressure of the gas, and carries with it all the deposit. The bottle is then immediately re-corked with a fresh cork, wired, foiled, and labelled, and is then ready for shipment. The degorgement can also be carried out without freezing the neck, by an expert " flip " of the bottle, as was the original method, and is still made use of to-day by some makers of Champagne.

Wines are coloured and/or sweetened by the addition of either " Colour Wine " or " Sweetening Wine ". The former is obtained by simmering down unfermented must until it is a deep brown colour, to which fully fermented wine is afterwards added. This forms with age a very sweet, dark product which is used for blending to produce " brown " wines.

Sweetening wine is used for sweetening blends other than brown wines, and is obtained by the addition of wine spirit to unfermented must, thus checking fermentation and retaining all the sugar of the grape.

In Burgundy, but not in Bordeaux, *chaptalisation* is practised. That is, cane or beet sugar may be added, if necessary, to the unfermented must to increase the sugar content, and so add to the ultimate alcoholic strength of the wine. German wines, also, are in certain circumstances " improved " by the addition of sugar.

In some cases *platrage* is resorted to. This is the addition of calcium sulphate to the must in order to increase the acidity of the wine, and is known in this country as "plastering". The acidity can also be increased by the addition of tartaric acid.

Mutage, in the form of sulphuring, is frequently carried out with white wines in order to check the fermentation and produce a sweet wine from grapes in which the sugar content is not sufficient to produce a naturally sweet wine. Such wines will of course have less alcoholic strength than those in which the fermentation ceases naturally.

After the pressing of the original wine, the "marc", that is, the skins and solid matter remaining in the press, can be pressed still further, sometimes with the addition of sugar or sugar and water, and inferior quality wines can be obtained therefrom. These are called *Vins de Presse* for the first pressing, which may be done with or without the addition of sugar, and *Vins de Marc* for the subsequent pressings with the addition of water. These wines are not generally offered for sale, but the distilled product called *Eau de Vie de Marc* very often is, although it requires a long period of maturation to become really palatable.

Sufficient has now been said concerning the broad principles of vinification. A whole book could be written upon the very many subtle modifications which are peculiar not only to the different wine-producing countries, but indeed to the separate districts of those countries.

Before concluding, mention must be made of the part that the type of grape and the soil and climatic conditions play in regard to the quality of the wine produced. The different countries and districts have found out by years of experience the type of grape which suits their conditions best, and the resulting wine is therefore very often inimitable, because usually the soil and the climate have the last word. For instance, the Muscat grape which in the South of France produces a rich, sweet wine, in the northern vignoble of Alsace produces a peculiarly dry wine. Similarly the Pedro Jimenez grape which in Spain one associates with a very sweet liqueur-like wine, produces a delightfully dry wine in the Hunter River area of Australia. Light gravelly and chalky soils in which it would be impossible to grow any other crop, suit the vine, whereas on a rich soil a large grape would be produced, of little use for wine-making, containing far too much water and lacking those qualities needed in a good wine grape.

Conditions of climate, including rainfall, sufficient sunshine to ripen the grapes, and the right conditions at the vintage, have restricted the areas of the world suitable for the cultivation of the grape for wine-making to two belts between the latitudes of 30 and 50 degrees North and South of the Equator. It is only those countries or, more correctly, the portions of those countries, which lie within these two belts that can produce fine wines.

Hitherto the wines of the Northern Hemisphere have proved the better, but there is no reason why, given time and similar experience, the cultivators of the Southern Hemisphere should not be able to produce at least as good wines as those of their northern competitors. So far the mass-production methods employed in the Empire wine-producing countries have tended to do away with the individual craftsman, and consequently with wines of an intimate character such as are produced by the individual vignerons of the Continent; but there is no reason why this state of affairs should remain for ever. Some connoisseurs are inclined to snort at the mention of Empire wines, but such prejudice is quite unwarranted, and a blindfold experiment in tasting might startle many of them, if confronted with some of the choicer Empire wines and asked to pick them out from amongst Continental ones of the same type.

2

DEFINITION OF THE TERM WINE

MUCH divergence of opinion is prevalent concerning the definition of the term wine, and what is, or is not, legitimately entitled to be described as such. Beverages consisting of the fermented products of parsnips and elderberries, for instance, are loosely described as home-made " wines ", and some brewers even fancifully describe their best brews as " barley wine ". The fermented products, made abroad, of such substances as palm juice, dates, bananas, and even mushrooms, are also designated " wines ".

Real wine is the fermented product of the *fruit of the vine*, hence the name, and any beverage not prepared mainly from fermented grapes is not wine, and is misnamed, if so called. The Wine and Spirit Association of this country has laid down the following definition: " Wine is the alcoholic beverage obtained by the fermentation of the juice of freshly gathered grapes, the fermentation of which has been carried out in the country of origin according to local traditions and practice."

In the opinion of the writer this description is too narrow in its application, precluding, as it does, those wines made in this country from dehydrated must and designated British

Wines. Such wines are the fermented product of the fruit of the vine, and as such, whatever their quality, are entitled to be described as wine. Of course it is quite possible to boil sultanas or raisins, ferment the products, and offer them as wines. Such beverages would certainly be the product of the fruit of the vine, but the concoctions resulting from such methods have nothing in common with beverages prepared from *fresh* grape juice, whether or not that juice has been subject to a process of dehydration. The point here is that true wine must be prepared from *fresh* grape juice, which the dehydrated concentrate used for the best British wine happens to be.

The term British Wine, however, is also unfortunately allowed to be applied to any alcoholic beverage made from fruit or sugar, or from a mixture of fruit and sugar, but the amending Act to the Labelling of Food Order (No. 2), 1944, requires such beverages to be labelled with an appropriate description and a *clear* indication of the fruit basis. Where this basis is exclusively grape juice, the appellation wine is a just description. In addition to the above categories, a blend, made in this country, of Empire and foreign wine, has also to be designated British Wine.

British wines have suffered in reputation in the past by the offering under that title of such atrocities as " Red Biddy ", but the tightening of the law now protects the public from such exploitation. The genuine British wine is a wholesome product, with a degree of quality equal to much that is of foreign origin. The popularity of these wines, probably owing to the preferential tariff enabling them to be sold comparatively cheaply, shows that they must at least possess some good qualities.

To many connoisseurs, the idea of the must being subjected to a process of dehydration (it has even been described as " mumification " by one such), is obnoxious in the extreme, and no amount of persuasion will convince them that the product of such a method can be at all palatable, and still less that it can be described as wine. The reader must decide this point for himself. It is not claimed here that these wines compare in any way with the *finest* of those produced in the countries of origin of the grape, but merely asserted that large quantities of alcoholic beverages are produced by the dehydration method, with a legitimate right to be called wine. On the other hand, what may be described as "fine wine" is produced by an entirely different method. The object of dehydration is merely to facilitate transport. It would be impossible to ship the freshly crushed grape juice, as the fermentation commences immediately the skin is broken, but the concentration of sugar in the dehydrated must is such that the action of the yeast germ is inhibited for the time being.

To revert to the Wine and Spirit Association's definition, and the words, "according to local traditions and practice": one might add that abroad there are many practices connected with vinification which would appear to be not less reprehensible than that of dehydration of the must, for instance, that of "mutage" mentioned previously. The processes of wine-making are as subtle as the commodity itself, and it would appear to be foolish to discriminate against any method in determining what may, or may not be, described as wine.

The term "non-alcoholic wine" is a misnomer, even when the product so described is obtained from grape juice, because wine is the *fermented* product of the grape, and as such *must* be alcoholic.

The alcoholic ginger, orange and raisin wines offered by the trade generally have a grape-juice basis with the addition of the flavouring, but cannot be regarded as true wines.

Medicated and Tonic wines, although having a real wine basis, are also not true wines because of the addition of the medicaments, and Vermouth, although made from a true wine basis, falls into the same category by reason of the addition of the various herbs, etc.

To sum up briefly: Wine is the fermented product of the *fresh* juice of the fruit of the vine (whatever the method of production), and not that of any other fruit, herb, grain or vegetable. This is the commonly accepted meaning of the term " real wine ".

3

STORAGE AND TREATMENT

A LARGE amount of hard work goes into the production of a bottle of wine, and much of this effort can be wasted if the wine subsequently receives improper treatment. The correct storage of one's purchases is therefore of vital importance if the best is to be obtained from them.

Temperature is an important factor. The best temperature in which to keep most wines is 54 degrees Fahr., but fortified wines can be subjected to 58-60 degrees without harm. It is not always easy to arrange for the correct temperature, but at least it should be aimed to keep the wine in an even temperature. For this purpose a cellar will usually prove the best place, because there the temperature will remain fairly constant. Draughts must be avoided at all costs, and the cellar should be dry, as dampness affects the corks. What harms wine most is extremes of heat and cold, and sudden changes of temperature, and these must be guarded against.

Vibration, and exposure to strong light are detrimental to some wines, notably Claret. Wines, therefore, should not be stored under stairs, or in similar places subject to vibration, nor should they be placed in a larder where sunlight may reach them. If no cellar is available, a quiet spot, free from vibration, and preferably in the dark, and where an even temperature is likely to be maintained, should be chosen.

Bottles of wine should always be stored on their sides, so as to allow the corks to be kept wet, and prevent any shrinkage of them, which would enable the air to get at the wine and spoil it. This, of course, only applies to wine in storage for any length of time; an upright position for a few days will do no harm. Champagne and other sparkling wines should *always* be kept in the prone position, as any shrinkage of the cork would allow the gas to escape and render the wine flat and insipid.

Wines should never be left in their cases, but unpacked and binned, so that the condition of the bottles can be examined from time to time. If it is not possible to unpack the cases immediately on delivery, they should be placed on the flat side and not stood on end. As the bottles are packed neck to punt, some of them would be upright and the corks not kept wet in the latter position.

Most wines, especially red wines, which have been stored for some time will have thrown a deposit, and great care must be taken to see that this is not disturbed. There is nothing unnatural about this deposit, and it is really a sign of the maturation of the wine. As a result of the storage of the bottles on their sides, this sediment or "crust" settles along the side of the bottle, and not at the bottom. For this reason unlabelled wines have a whitewash brush drawn across the punt end of the bottles as they are being binned by the merchant, in order to show which side of the bottle should be kept uppermost when it is being handled in a horizontal position. Labelled wines are of course binned with the label uppermost. Wines should not be handled unnecessarily, but left quietly resting until the time for their opening and decanting arrives. If wines of this description have been recently transported from the wine merchant, and are required for consumption fairly soon, it is best to stand them up for twenty-four hours, when the sediment will sink to the bottom. The wine must then be carefully decanted. When, however, such wines are needed for *immediate* consumption, it is best to ask the wine merchant supplying them to decant them first.

Wines in storage should be frequently examined for any " weepers ", that is, bottles from which there is a slight leakage from the cork. Such wines should be consumed early before deterioration sets in.

It is important that no cask vinegar be stored in the same cellar as bottled wines, as it may affect them.

When binning a few bottles on a shelf, make sure that no slipping can take place, by placing wedges at the sides. There should be two at each side of the stack. These wedges can easily be cut from an old cork with a sharp knife or razor blade. If a wire bin with separate compartments for each bottle can be obtained this will be found to be the better arrangement.

Very little divergence of opinion exists upon the question of the storage of wine, and most connoisseurs will agree with the foregoing remarks. There is, however, a considerable difference of opinion concerning the service of wine, which is dealt with in Chapter 6.

4

THE CHOICE OF WINE

THIS subject raises, for the more fortunate, the question of cellar stocking, but it is not intended to discuss this aspect of the matter here because the needs of one individual would be entirely different from those of another. Any advice regarding the stocking of a cellar should be sought from a reputable wine merchant, when such matters as available accommodation, personal tastes, extent of entertaining and, above all, the expense to which one is prepared to go, could be discussed over a glass of sherry, when a far more satisfactory conclusion would be arrived at than any amount of written instruction could provide.

However, if it is only a question of having a few bottles in hand to meet the ordinary emergencies, a bottle or two of dry Sherry, a good Port, and a few bottles each of white Bordeaux, Claret, and Burgundy would be sufficient for this purpose. The possession of some Champagne, also, would place the owner in a position to meet almost any demands upon his hospitality.

The real intention of this chapter is to discuss what, to some, is still a bewildering question, that of which wine should accompany each particular dish.

Many people might reply that any wine one enjoys is the wine to have—but the matter is not quite so simple as that. A good dish can easily be spoiled by taking the wrong wine with it, just as a fine wine can be utterly ruined if accompanied by the wrong dish. But this is not the only consideration. It

is of the greatest importance, in selecting a wine, to think also of those which have preceded, or are to follow it. It is, however, quite easy to remember the few basic rules which resolve the whole matter into one of extreme simplicity.

Generally speaking, wine should always be accompanied by, or precede food—Champagne and Sherry excepted. These two wines are quite acceptable unaccompanied, although both also find their place in the menu.

Sherry is a wine suitable for nearly all occasions. It does not deteriorate in the decanter, and it is alleged by some not to be prejudiced by smoking, but this, of course, is a matter of taste. It may be offered to the unexpected guest at almost any time of the day.

Champagne at 11 o'clock in the morning is excellent, but this indulgence is not within the means of everyone. It is generally accepted as the wine for special occasions such as birthdays, christenings and weddings, and as it represents, to a great extent, the acme of the winemaker's art, such relegation is not out of place.

A glass of Port with a biscuit, and a Madeira (the full

variety) with a slice of cake, are also suitable for entertaining the unexpected guest.

The generally accepted sequence of alcoholic drinks with a meal is an aperitif *before* the repast; followed by beverage wines chosen according to the dishes they are to accompany; a dessert wine after the sweet; with a liqueur or old Brandy accompanying the coffee, but preferably drunk after it. The aperitif may take the form of Vermouth, or one of the recognised proprietary aperitifs such as Lillet, or a light dry Sherry such as a Fino is very suitable, especially on occasions when fine wines are to follow. A dry Sherry does not destroy the palate for the proper appreciation of any delicate wines served later.

Wines must be chosen with a view to presenting them in a crescendo from the light, dry and delicate ones up to the strong, sweet and full-bodied varieties.

The French (who no one can deny are more gastronomically minded than perhaps any other nation), serve Port as an aperitif before a meal. This may be perfectly correct from a gastronomic point of view, but surely not from a vinous one. Probably the interpolation of the hors d'œuvre (if not too highly condimented), serves to clean the palate before the introduction of more delicate wines, but the writer would still prefer to keep to his Sherry. However, Messrs. Cockburn have recently introduced a *dry* white aperitif Port, so now the whole matter appears to be satisfactorily settled!

The average person is not usually concerned with the organisation of a banquet where different wines are to be served with each course, but if he is ever confronted with such a task he would do well to consult the proposed supplier, who, being thoroughly conversant with the qualities of his own wines, will be able to assist more than anyone in their correct presentation. What is more often the concern of the ordinary individual is the choice of the correct wine to accompany the *main* dish of a meal. The directions given at the end of this chapter should make this a comparatively simple task.

For a not too formal meal the ideal service would consist of dry Sherry before the meal—the hors d'œuvre and soup should then need no accompaniment; a grand fine wine served with the main dish; followed by a tawny or vintage Port with the dessert; and with the coffee a rare old Brandy, or, for the ladies, a liqueur.

Champagne makes an ideal wine when one only is being served throughout the meal, because it goes well with any dish. Also it is usually difficult to fit this wine in with others, and consequently it is best served alone. Port and Champagne do not, however, accord, so it is best to choose a rich Madeira, or rich Sherry as a dessert wine after Champagne—this, of course, is again a matter of opinion.

Wine cannot be properly appreciated with dishes that are accompanied by vinegar, horseradish, pickles, or piquant sauces. For these it is best to choose beer, and for curried dishes, lager beer, and to dispense with wine altogether on such occasions.

Red wines should never accompany oysters or fish, because these wines contain a large amount of tannin, which prevents the proper digestion of fish foods.

When purchasing wine for entertaining or for one's own requirements, it must always be remembered that the natural beverage wines, being low in alcoholic strength, cannot be expected to keep in *perfect* condition for more than a few hours after opening. The purchase of a few half bottles will therefore prove a matter of economy, but as wine develops better the larger the bottle, the splitting of a whole bottle between two persons is to be recommended.

With the Australian burgundy-type wines supplied in the screw-stopper flagons, no deterioration apears to take place even a week or so after opening, provided the stopper has been replaced securely, but of course these wines cannot be regarded as " great " wines. The same thing may not be expected from the Grand Cru French wines, though this too is debatable, because some authorities are now asserting that good beverage wines should keep for forty-eight hours at least. The writer is, however, still of the opinion that although such wine may be drinkable, it could never be up to the standard of that taken from a freshly opened bottle.

For the purpose of estimating requirements, allow one bottle of beverage wine for two persons (where only one wine is being served). With dessert wines the average bottle provides about ten glasses.

The diversity of character in wines demands a careful study in making the choice of the order in which they should be served, and the following notes, based upon the experience of generations of wine drinkers, are appended as a guide. There is no reason why they should be slavishly followed, but the uninitiated would do well to be guided by them, at any rate at first, and make any experiments later.

HORS D'OEUVRE

These are nearly always inimical to wine because of their pickled or highly condimented nature, but those that are simply made and are little more than a vehicle for olive oil are best accompanied by Sherry. Grape fruit or melon can be substituted, the former with a few drops of Sherry on it, the latter accompanied by a sweet wine, but either will probably upset the rest of the vinous programme.

On occasions when fine wines are to follow, caviare or oysters may be chosen. The former needs no accompanying wine, with the latter any dry white wine may be served, Chablis being the popular choice, but be sure that it is real Chablis.

SOUP

Good soup really needs no accompanying wine, but if one prefers it, dry Sherry may be served. Young Hock or Moselle goes well with bisques, especially if other German wines are to follow. Dry Madeira (Verdelho) is the recognised wine to serve with turtle soup. Germiny is too acid a soup for the introduction of fine wine, and mulligatawny kills wine.

FISH

This should *never* be accompanied by red wine. Mornay sauce served with fish assists wine. White French or German dry or semi-dry wines are the best accompaniments, or a rosé

wine may be used. Lobster goes well with Chablis or other white Burgundy, or with Champagne when no red wine is to follow. Smoked salmon is best accompanied by medium dry Graves, or Hock, especially the latter.

ROAST JOINTS

Serve Claret or Burgundy, but veal goes well with any white wine. Mint sauce served with lamb is fatal to any wine.

POULTRY

Plainly cooked birds are best accompanied by Claret or Burgundy, but if elaborately stuffed, choose Hock or Champagne. Rhône wine is the best accompaniment to duck. White wine is best with cold chicken.

GAME

Burgundy with pheasant, Claret (preferably St. Emilion) with partridge, Claret (red Graves preferably) with grouse, but Hock or Moselle with it when cold. With woodcock serve the greatest red wine available.

The salads accompanying the above should be free from vinegar.

VEGETABLES

Most vegetables neither help nor hinder wine, but carrots, by reason of their sweetness, are detrimental to dry white wines. Spinach and turnip tops are better with dry rather than semi-sweet wines. Mushrooms are excellent with all wines.

SWEETS

These are best unaccompanied by wine, but sweet wines such as Sauternes or Tokay may be served. Dishes flavoured with liqueurs are inimical to wine.

CHEESE

This goes well with any red wine, but does not accord with semi-acid light white wines, as it makes them appear thin and sharp.

With Stilton, vintage Port of course, but with Brie vintage Claret may be served in lieu. Camembert, Roquefort and Cheshire are all best with tawny Port.

FRUIT AND NUTS

Fruit is best unaccompanied by wine, but strawberries accord well with Port. Apples may be accompanied by Burgundy or Claret if desired, and cherries, grapes, peaches and pears, by Hock or Sauternes. Oranges do not accord with wine.

Nuts accord with most wines, but best of all with old Port, brown Sherry or rich Madeira.

SUNDRIES

Egg dishes do not usually accord with wine because of their sulphur content.

Curried dishes are completely inimical to wine.

Ham is best accompanied by white rather than red wine.

Spaghetti and macaroni dishes are usually accompanied by Chianti.

Generally, red table wine may be served with red meat, and white table wine with white meat. White wine is best with cold poultry.

Where two or more wines of the same type have been chosen, the younger wine should be served before the older, unless the latter is not of such a good year. The whole object in serving should be to prevent the more delicate wines from being unappreciated, owing to the previous dulling of the palate by a stronger and sweeter wine. Usually white wine should be served before red, but not a sweet white wine before a dry red, everything of course depending on the individual wines.

Amongst other factors governing the choice of wines, is that of the vintage. This is being made the subject of the following chapter.

RESUME

Hors d'Œuvre	Dry Sherry, dry Moselle, or dry Alsatian.
Soup	Dry Madeira, or dry Sherry.
Fish	Dry Champagne, dry Graves, dry Hock, dry white Burgundy, dry Moselle, or dry Alsatian.
Entrees	Red Bordeaux, red Burgundy, or red Côtes-du-Rhône.
Roast or Bird	Claret, red Burgundy, or red Rhône wine, but white wine may be served with cold poultry.

SWEETS	Sweet Champagne, sweet Hock or Moselle, Sauternes, or sweet Tokay (but really best unaccompanied).
CHEESE	Red Bordeaux or red Burgundy, red Côtes-du-Rhône, vintage Claret, vintage or tawny Port.
DESSERT	Sweet Madeira, Port, brown Sherry, sweet Rhine, Sauternes, or sweet Tokay.

ITALIAN WINES AND THE MENU

No Italian wines have been included in the above. If such are preferred the following can be substituted:

For	
For *Burgundy* . . .	Barolo or Barolino
Claret	Chianti or red Capri
Dry white wine . .	White Capri
Semi-sweet white wine .	Orvieto, Falerno, Lachryma Christi
Champagne . . .	Asti Spumante
Sherry	Marsala
Dessert wine . . .	Moscato or Malvasia

As a further help in arriving at the best wine to choose for any particular dish, a guide to the *style* of wine which should accompany the various dishes is appended. Charts, showing the styles of the French wines, and of ports and sherries, are also given.

GUIDE TO THE STYLE OF WINE TO ACCOMPANY EACH DISH

DRY WHITE OR ROSE (slightly cooled)	SWEET WHITE OR ROSE (very cool)
Oysters	Asparagus
Other shellfish	Vol-au-vent
Fish	Sweetbread (or red if preferred)
White meat	Lamb (or red if preferred)
Pork-butcher's meat	Mushrooms (or red if preferred)
Ham (or red if preferred)	Truffles (or red if preferred)
Poultry (or red if preferred)	

SWEET LIQUEUR WINES

(very cold)

Foie-gras
Biscuits
Petits fours
Desserts

LIGHT RED WINE

(room temperature)

	Cheeses
Lamb	Brie
Sweetbread	Port Salut
Veal	Dutch
Ham	Reblochon
Chicken	
Turkey	
Grouse	
Pigeon	
Quail	
Partridge	
Lark	
Thrush	

FULL-BODIED RED

(room temperature)

	Cheeses
Beef	Roquefort
Pork	Emmenthal
Mutton	Gruyere
Duck	Cheshire
Goose	Munster
Guinea fowl	Camembert
Braised meat	
Wild boar	
Venison	
Hare	
Pheasant	
Woodcock	
Pies	
Truffles	
Mushrooms	

(Camembert, Roquefort and Cheshire cheeses also go well with tawny Port. Stilton is best accompanied by vintage Port.)

GUIDE TO STYLES OF FRENCH WHITE WINES

DRY

(containing no sugar)

Chablis
Château Châlon
White Burgundies of:
 Fixin, Pernand Vergelesses, Laidox-Serrigny, Savigny-les-Beaune, Auxey-Duresses, St. Aubin, Santenay, Montagny, Rully, Mercurey, Macon Blanc.
Brut Champagne

STRONG SWEET

(rich in alcohol and sugar)

Barsac (some)
Sauternes (some)
Loupiac (some)
Ste. Croix-du-Mont (some)
Anjou (some)
Vouvray (some)
Monbazillac

DRY OR LIGHTLY SOFT

Bordeaux:
 Graves (some)
 Premières Côtes (some)
 Bordeaux (some)
 Bordeaux Supérieur (some)
 Bourg
 Blaye
 Côtes St. Macaire

SWEET OR VERY SWEET

Bordeaux:
 Graves (some)
 Premières Côtes (most)
 Bordeaux (some)
 Bordeaux Supérieur (some)
 Cerons
 Loupiac
 Ste. Croix-du-Mont

DRY OR LIGHTLY SOFT
(contd.)

Entre-deux-Mers
Graves de Vayres

Burgundy:
Montrachet
Meursault
Blagny
Pouilly-Fuissé
Corton
Charlemagne
Musigny
Blanc de Vougeot
Côte de Beaune

Alsace:
Riesling
Traminer
Gewurtztraminer
Tokay
Sylvaner

Rhône:
Condrieu
Hermitage
St. Peray
Châteauneuf-du-Pape

Others:
Anjou (some)
Saumur (some)
Vouvray (some)
Pouilly-Fumé
Bergerac (some)
Montravel (some)

Champagne:
Dry

SWEET OR VERY SWEET
(contd.)

Ste. Foy Bordeaux
Barsac and Sauternes

Others:
Anjou (some)
Saumur (some)
Vouvray (some)

Bergerac (some)
Montravel (some)

Champagne:
Demi-sec

GUIDE TO STYLES OF FRENCH RED WINES

LIGHT-BODIED AND DELICATE

Bordeaux:
Bordeaux and Bordeaux Supérieur
Blaye
Médoc and Haut-Médoc (especially Margaux)

Burgundy:
Beaujolais (some)

Others:
Bourgeuil
Chinon

FULL-BODIED

Bordeaux:
- St. Emilion (some)
- Pomerol (some)

Burgundy:
- Chambertin
- Clos de la Perrière
- Clos de Vougeot
- Corton
- Clos de Tart

Burgundy (cont.):
- Clos de la Roche
- Clos St. Denis
- Bonnes Mares
- St. Georges
- Richebourg
- Santenots

Rhône:
- Châteauneuf-du-Pape

MORE FULL-BODIED

Bordeaux:
- St. Emilion
- Pomerol
- Fronsac
- Bourg
- Graves (especially Haut-Brion)
- Haut-Médoc (especially Pauillac and Moulis)

Beaujolais:
- Morgon
- Brouilly
- Moulin-à-Vent

Burgundy:
- Musigny
- The Romanée wines
- Grands Echezeaux
- Côtes de Beaune
- Volnay
- Monthélie
- Santenay
- Mercurey

Rhône:
- Hermitage
- Côte-Rôtie

GUIDE TO THE STYLES OF PORT

RUBY These are blends which have been kept in wood for some years before bottling. They lose some of their depth of colour whilst in the wood, but will have more body and colour than Tawny. They throw a crust in course of time.

TAWNY Tawny ports are blends which have been maturing in wood for a considerable number of years. Thus treated, they lose their depth of colour and take on a rust-like tinge. They are usually expensive because of the large amount of evaporation taking place during maturation, but they have a compensating delicacy and mellowness.

They are intended for early use after bottling, and should not be laid down as they will go to pieces rather than throw a crust, having already completed their maturation. Cheap Tawny Ports should be avoided, as they will probably only be blends of young white and red Ports.

VINTAGE These are the wines of *one* year, bottled when about two years old, and allowed to mature in bottle. By being bottled early they retain their vintage character, full-bodied, deep ruby colour, and fine bouquet. During the process of maturation they throw the well-known crust.

OLD CRUSTED These are blends of young wines of *different* years, shipped in cask like the Vintage and allowed to mature in bottle in the same way. They will throw a crust like a Vintage Port, and although probably not up to the same standard, will approximate it in character, and they are usually less expensive.

LATE-BOTTLED VINTAGE These vintage wines are kept in wood for some ten to fifteen years before bottling. They will be lighter in colour than the ordinary Vintage, but after they have been in bottle for some time will develop a bouquet that no Tawny wine would have.

WHITE This is made from white grapes. It is never bottled early, but is matured in wood, and is nearly always very sweet. It never throws a firm crust, and is therefore not suitable for laying down. White Port is not favoured as much as the red.

GUIDE TO THE STYLES OF SHERRY

Sherries can be divided into two classes, those which have developed " flor ", and those which have not. Flor is a white organic growth which forms upon the surface of some maturing sherries, and which converts some of the alcohol into aldehyde, giving character to the wine.

FINO Very dry pale wine with a clean finish. It makes a fine aperitif. It is one in which the flor has been allowed to develop.

AMONTILLADO Less dry than Fino but with a fine bouquet. It is a result of further development of the Fino.

MONTILLA Very dry wine in a class by itself, produced near Cordova. (The term Amontillado, used above, actually means, " made like Montilla ".)

MANZANILLA The dryest of all with an almost bitter finish. It is made near the sea, which is alleged to give the wine its character.

VINO DE PASTO This is a wine of no great character, being an ordinary golden wine. The name means " table wine ".

GOLDEN A medium rich wine in which the flor has not developed.

AMOROSO This is a term used for a rather sweet Oloroso style, and is not a Spanish term.

OLOROSO This is a nutty-flavoured wine in which the flor has not developed or has been checked. The wine may be dry or rich, the latter making an excellent dessert wine.

BROWN A full rich wine which has been coloured and sweetened.

OLD EAST INDIA A term given to a style of wine which was formerly shipped to the East. Generally a medium dry wine of characteristic style.

SACK Old English name for Sherry. Wines offered under this name are usually dry.

CREAM SHERRY This is usually a blend of old Fino and old Oloroso.

BRISTOL MILK This term arose from the blending of Sherry at this port in the past. To-day the name is usually associated with proprietary brands of a golden style. Bristol Cream is a full pale wine.

Much good Sherry is offered under fancy Spanish-sounding names, which have no real meaning in that language. Such wines usually have their style described by the addition of one or other of the above terms. The best guarantee of the quality of a Sherry is that of the name of the shipper.

5

VINTAGE WINES

THIS is a subject about which much ignorance exists, a lot of so-called knowledge is aired, and much snobbishness displayed.

The actual interpretation of the word vintage varies in connection with the different types of wine. In the case of the natural beverage wines it not only indicates that the wine is of one particular year, but *also* that it is of one particular vineyard without the addition of any other wine—neither of the same year but from another vineyard, nor from the same vineyard but of a different year.

In the case of blended wines such as Port and Champagne, " vintage " only indicates that the wine is of that particular year alone, without the addition of the wine of any former year. It will be the wine of that year drawn from many different vineyards.

Sherry, the production of which necessitates the blending of wines of former years, is not concerned with vintage dates. It is quite possible to produce Vintage Sherry, and this is sometimes done, but it is not the general custom to do so, nor to offer such for sale.

The vagaries of the climate on the continent of Europe materially affect the quality of the wine produced from year to year, so that vintage dates in connection with certain Continental wines are a matter of some importance. The Italians, however, are not vintage-minded, consequently vintage dates do not often appear on the labels of their wines.

Empire wine-producing countries enjoy a fairly constant

climate, so that vintage dates do not matter to anything like the same extent as they do in Europe. Moreover, owing to the mass-production methods employed and the standardisation of the wines ensuing from such methods, vintage dates have hitherto not entered into the realm of Empire wines. In recent years, however, some shippers of these wines have begun to declare vintages, and although not much has yet been published concerning the merits of the various years, the inclusion of a date on the label does at least indicate the age of the wine.

Vintage dates must always be read in conjunction with the name of the estate or the shipper offering the wine. Many a mediocre wine is made in a " good " year by those vignerons who place quantity before quality, and although the inclusion upon the label of the date of a good year may be perfectly legitimate and honest, the wine may be anything but a " fine " wine. In the case of Burgundy, the name of the shipper is of supreme importance, owing to the fact that the vineyards producing this wine are mostly divided amongst many different owners. Because of this, it is quite possible to have wines of the same estate and the same year varying in quality, according to the skill and commercial integrity of the particular vignerons who produced them. The name of the shipper who has *selected* the wine is, therefore, probably of greater importance than the vintage date.

In the case of Champagne also, the year is probably less important than the name of the shipper-producer. Good shippers only declare a vintage when their own particular wine merits it, and should their wine of any particular year be deficient in certain qualities, will then blend it with a suitable wine of a former year, and only offer it as a non-vintage wine. But the less reputable shipper, taking advantage of the fact that the year is an exceptional one as a whole, will be only too pleased to display that date whether his wine is of any special merit or not.

There are many persons who regard a non-vintage Champagne as something inferior, but this is certainly not true of the wine of reputable shippers, which in most cases is a very fine wine indeed but has not been declared a vintage one for the very sound and honest reason that, in order to *improve* its quality, it has been blended with wine of a former year. Moreover, as under the French law only 80% of any Champagne vintage is allowed to be sold under the "*Millésime*", it follows that the remainder, even in the most exceptional years, must find its way into the non-vintage wines.

The non-vintage wines of the leading shippers, therefore, will usually prove to be better value than the vintage ones of some little-known brand. The whole art of Champagne-making depends on the skill of the blender, and the leading shippers have only gained their reputation by their skill and experience.

Another pitfall for the unwary in considering vintage dates is connected with the knowledge of the development of the various wines. Although, by reference to a chart, the year appearing on the label of a bottle may prove to be an "exceptional" one, the wine may still be inferior owing to one or other of two factors: it may have matured quickly and be past its prime when offered, or it may be only slowly developing and have not yet reached the stage when the bottle should be opened. A knowledge of how the wine of any particular vintage is behaving is therefore absolutely necessary in order to ensure that the year selected is the right one.

It must also be remembered that the date appearing on the label of a wine is that of the actual vintage (gathering of the grapes), and that the wine has generally to spend between two and three years in cask before being ready for bottling, and even *then* is usually not fit to drink. It is not reasonable, therefore, to expect a 1947 wine of the nature, say, of a Claret to be ready for drinking in 1950, but the same would not apply to a Beaujolais.

There is also the question of the length of life that can be expected from the various types of wine. White wines usually lack the longevity of red wines, but some, such as the Vins Jaunes of the Jura, and the Hungarian Tokay, are extremely long-lived. Generally, good Claret will last from forty to seventy years, Burgundy is not so long-lived, and the Beaujolais Burgundies are best drunk young for they possess no longevity. Champagne is usually at its prime when between ten and twelve years and cannot be safely relied upon after fifteen years, but wines which have been treated carefully very often last longer, especially if bottled in magnums.

Hocks and Moselles are comparatively short-lived, twelve to fifteen years is about the maximum for the majority, and although " Trockenbeerenauslese " wines can last very many years, they do not usually show any further improvement after fifteen years.

Ports age slowly and it is impossible to say how long a good Vintage Port will last, but Tawny Port is ready to drink when bottled, and will not keep too long, having already matured many years in the wood.

Sherry gains little from being kept, and like Tawny Port has spent many years in cask before being bottled.

Bearing all these facts in mind, it may be asked " How is the layman correctly to choose the right wine?" The answer is simple. Let him purchase his requirements from a reputable wine merchant and rely on the experience and judgment of the latter; or, if dining out, use a restaurant with a reputation for its wine list. In both cases there will still be room for the use and practice of individual knowledge, in making a choice from the suggestions of the experts. The wines listed by a reputable wine merchant or hotel restaurant will have been chosen solely for their choiceness and suitability for current consumption. Of course wine merchants often have wines to offer which are only suitable for laying down, but in such cases this will always be explained to the would-be purchaser.

Finally, it is not wise to insist on a vintage wine for every occasion. There is not the least doubt that Vintage Port is the supreme representative of this type of wine, but Tawny Port also has much in its favour. Indeed, the leading Port shippers will very often miss declaring a vintage, preferring to keep their wine to augment the standard of their Tawny. Also, as has already been mentioned, non-vintage Champagne of a good shipper is really first-class wine. It cannot therefore be over emphasised that to insist upon always having a wine with a date is to deny oneself the benefit of much good wine. It is more important to see that the wine is that of a good shipper.

For the benefit of those who would like such information, a chart of the supreme vintages of the last half-century is given on the two following pages, showing the minimum time from the vintage (date on the bottle) that each type of wine requires to develop in order to be drinkable, and the approximate normal life of the wine. As, however, the same wines vary in their development with each vintage, even such a chart is apt to be misleading to the uninitiated. For instance, the 1911, 1924, and 1929 Clarets are now past their best, and many more of the white Bordeaux wines are in the same category. It must also be remembered that many excellent wines are made in normal years, and some good ones even in poor years.

VINTAGE GUIDE TO LAST HALF-CENTURY

Wine	*Minimum Time to Mature from V. Date*	*Approximate Normal Life*	*Superlative Vintage Years*[1]	*Poor Years*
Vintage Port	10 years preferably 12 years	Indefinite	1900, 1904, 1908, 1912, 1917, 1919, 1920, 1922, 1924, *1927*, 1934, 1935, 1938, *1942*, 1945, *1947*, 1948, 1950	1905, 1913, 1918, 1932, 1944
Champagne	5 years	10-15 years	1921, *1928*, 1929, 1934, 1937, 1942, 1943, 1945, *1947*, 1949	1922, 1925, 1927, 1930, 1931, 1932
Bordeaux, Red	5 years	40-50 years Depends on development	1900, 1904, 1911, 1914, 1920, *1921*, 1924, *1928*, 1929, 1934, 1937, *1945*, 1947, 1949, 1950	1915, 1922, 1927, 1930, 1931, 1932, 1935, 1939, 1941
Bordeaux, White (Sauternes)	5 years 5 years	Not so long as red (20-40 years)	1900, 1904, 1906, *1921*, 1928, *1929*, 1934, 1937, 1943, *1945*, 1947, 1949	1915, 1918, 1925, 1930, 1931, 1932, 1935, 1941

[1] Dates in italics indicate the very best years.

BURGUNDY, RED	5 years	10-20 years, some longer	1904, 1906, 1911, 1915, 1923, 1928, 1929, 1933, 1934, *1945*, *1947*	1922, 1925, 1927, 1930, 1931, 1932, 1939, 1941, 1944
(Beaujolais)	(2½ years)	(at best 3-4 Max. 10 years)		
BURGUNDY, WHITE	5 years	10-15 years	1921, 1923, 1928, *1929*, 1933, 1934, 1937, 1942, 1943, 1945, *1947*	1925, 1927, 1930, 1931, 1932, 1939, 1941, 1944
(Chablis)	(3-4 years)	(at best 4-5)		
ALSACE	best young	10-12 years	*1921*, 1929, 1934, 1937, 1943, *1947*	1922, 1927, 1930, 1931, 1939, 1944
ANJOU	best young	but white long lived	1900, *1921*, 1923, 1929, 1933, *1945*, *1947*	1922, 1927, 1941, 1944
RHONE (Tavel)	4 years (best young)	10-20 years (not long)	1923, 1924, 1928, *1929*, 1933, 1934, 1937, 1943, *1945*, 1946, 1947, 1949	1927
HOCK	best young	12-15 years, some longer	1915, 1920, *1921*, 1929, 1933, 1934, 1937, 1942, 1943, 1945, 1947, 1948, 1949	1919, 1926, 1939, 1941
MOSELLE	best young	10-12 years		
COGNAC	3-4 years cask age	Indefinite, no in-bottle improvement	1900, *1906*, *1919*, 1920, 1928, *1929*, 1943, 1947 (Quality depending on cask age)	1901, 1902, 1915, 1930, 1932

6

SERVICE OF WINE

THIS chapter is concerned with the correct presentation of wine at the table. It is in the final service of wine that probably the greatest risk of spoiling it occurs.

The order of service is of paramount importance, and this has already been fully dealt with in the chapter concerning the Choice of Wine.

Most wines are best served decanted, but this again is a matter where much divergence of opinion exists, and is the subject of a separate chapter, as is also the vexed question of the appropriate glass.

The treatment of red wines in the matter of service is usually different from that of the white. Generally, red beverage wines should be served at room temperature. They should therefore be decanted and brought up from the cellar some three hours before being required, and left to take the temperature naturally. The French expression for this is *chambrer*. The wines should never be placed in warm water or near a fire in an attempt to hasten the process, it being far better to serve them at the lower temperature, and allow the warmth of the hand around the individual glass to bring out the bouquet. If the wine has not been decanted, but has been brought up in the bottles, the corks should be drawn about one hour before the wine is required, to allow it to " breathe " and expand.

Some connoisseurs consider that whilst Claret is best served at room temperature, red Rhône wine is better at a temperature cool enough to produce on the palate an invigorating sense of freshness. Burgundy, it is also conceded, should be drunk at a lower temperature than Claret, that is, only slightly above cellar temperature, so that Rhône and Burgundy wines need only be brought up about one hour before they are required, and, if not decanted, the corks should be drawn.

Dessert wines are generally served at room temperature, and hitherto this has been the invariable rule for Port. Recently, however, chilled *Tawny* Port has been served with some success as an aperitif, the bottles being placed for about one hour unopened in a refrigerator at a temperature of 39-40 degrees Fahr. Such treatment, however, would not be applicable to a Vintage Port.

White and rosé wines are usually served at cellar temperature, and therefore need not be brought up until just before they are required. Some people prefer these wines iced, and the following may be served chilled if desired: dry sparkling wines, dry sherry, Vermouth, white Rhône, Hock and Moselle, Vouvray, white Burgundy, still Champagne and Graves.

The following may be served *very cold:* sweet sparkling wines, rosé wines, and sweet French, Italian and Hungarian dessert wines.

Usually the wines of high alcoholic content can be enjoyed at a lower temperature than those of lower alcoholic strength, but *all* white wines are best served cold. A truly dry Champagne, however, does not *need* to be iced. The effect of icing sweet wines is to conceal to a certain extent the sweetness.

In icing a delicate wine, it should be done gradually, by first wrapping a wet cloth around the bottle, and later a cloth dipped in ice water, finally placing the bottle in the ice bucket just before serving. The French expression for a wine iced sufficiently to bring out the qualities, is *frappé.*

In serving wine, never add the contents of one bottle of the same wine to that of another, neither in the decanter nor in the individual glass, as by so doing any individuality of the particular bottle will be lost.

In restaurants, it is customary for the wine waiter first to pour a little of the wine ordered into the host's glass, so that the latter may sample it and signify his approval of the bottle before its contents are served to his guests. This is called " Taking the Say " (*assaye*).

Port is usually passed round the " way of the sun ", that is from the host's left hand back to his right hand. This, of course, has no mystical influence upon the bouquet of the wine, but it is an old custom that many lovers of wine prefer to maintain.

Smoking should not take place whilst fine wines are being served, as no wine can be fully appreciated in an atmosphere of smoke, and it is a courtesy due to others that indulgence in the weed should be postponed at any rate until the coffee stage is reached.

Many books on the subject of wine continually refer to the incompetence of the average wine waiter. This is unfair to a degree. There is certainly room for improvement in the service of wine in this country, and no doubt the formation of the Guild of Sommeliers will do much to remedy this, but generally wine waiters are not half so bad as they are painted. Of course those restaurants where one is asked whether one would like the Claret iced, should not be visited a second time!

The writer's main objection to the average restaurant service is that wines which require decanting are never thus served. Considering the prices which are usually charged, this little extra service could easily be arranged. Generally the bottle is fetched from the cellar and held at an almost vertical angle for one's inspection, presumably to ensure that the order has been taken correctly. The bottle is then whisked off, and no one knows to how much further movement it is subjected before reappearing in the inevitable cradle. By this time a thorough disturbance of the crust has resulted, and the last to be served, which is of course the host, suffers in consequence. Another annoying habit in the majority of restaurants is that of producing the wine when the dish which it should have accompanied is already half consumed. A good tip when dining out is, if possible, to telephone the hotel and choose the wine in advance, when it can be served *chambrer* or *frappé* at the right moment, and according to one's instructions.

7

DECANTING

THE question of whether to decant or not to decant is a very vexed one. There can be no argument, however, concerning the fact that this method of presentation of a wine at table has much in its favour. A decanter will always have a better appearance than a bottle, showing up the colour of the wine, scintillating in the light, and harmonising with the silver and the decorations. Where a wine has thrown a crust, decanting, or some alternative, is essential, as any attempt to pour from the bottle would result in the deposit fouling the wine, by reason of the backwash.

Some connoisseurs, however, are adverse to the decanting of fine wines on the score that too much of the surface of the wine is exposed to the air in the process, with consequent loss of bouquet. Such persons prefer to serve from the cradle, but even then there is bound to be a slight backwash and consequent disturbance of the crust, and one sometimes experiences this when dining out. The use of a silver funnel for directing the wine down the side of the decanter, and thus avoiding frothing, will usually serve to prevent any undue exposure to the air. The real object of the cradle is for convenience in decanting.

When a bottle is being removed from a bin for decanting, the horizontal position should be maintained and the bottle placed gently in the cradle. The cork can then be carefully drawn by placing the cradle on a table, and firmly holding down the bottle with the left hand whilst the cork is being drawn. This drawing should be done without any jerkiness. The wine should then be carefuly poured into a clean decanter until all the bright wine has been drawn off, care being taken to stop as soon as any sediment approaches the neck of the bottle. A light behind the neck (candle or bulb) is nearly always essential.

Before drawing the cork, all portions of the wax or capsule should be removed, and the top of the cork and neck of the bottle should be carefully wiped. The mouth of the bottle should be wiped again after the cork has been drawn, before pouring out the wine. It is essential, of course, to use a perfectly clean cloth for this purpose. With a recalcitrant cork recourse to the pincers will have to be made. These should be heated until just glowing and then applied to the neck of the bottle just below the cork, for about a quarter of a minute. After this a piece of twine or a feather dipped in water is applied to the exact place where the pincers rested, when the neck will come off quite cleanly together with the imprisoned cork.

The correct type of corkscrew to use with wine bottles is the wire variety with a generously spaced spiral. The narrow gimlet type is no use and more often than not pulls right through the cork. With age, the cork of a wine bottle hardens, and the lower portion being wider than the top, can only be extracted by a long, strong, and steady pull, avoiding any jerks which would, of course, disturb the deposit.

Decanters should be throughly clean and *dry* before the wine is poured into them, and should be large enough to take the whole of the wine, as no pause can be made once pouring has commenced. They should also be at the right temperature, that of the wine. When cleansing decanters, all forms of scouring preparations should be avoided. The decanters should be rinsed with warm water, and any deposit from previous contents should be removed by the use of small shot. Some people object to the use of decanters on the grounds that if improperly cleansed they may give a taint to the wine, but then of course the same argument might apply to the use of glasses. Again, there are others who, although agreeing with the necessity for decanting, prefer to bring the bottle up from the cellar first and leave it standing upright, only decanting just before serving. There seems to be no great advantage in this, because the crust, having been allowed to slip, is more likely to mingle with the wine in the process of decanting than if no disturbance had been allowed to take place. Certainly, if one can be sure of the deposit *remaining* in the punt of the bottle, there will be less of it in contact with the surface of the wine, but usually the less disturbance of the crust that can be made, the better.

Of course, when a wine with a deposit has recently been transported, for instance, from the wine merchant, and is required for consumption fairly soon, it will *have* to be stood up and the sediment allowed to settle before decanting. This settlement will in all probability take as long as twenty-four hours. When buying vintage Port for immediate use, the wine merchant should be asked to decant it into fresh bottles, which he will gladly do.

Some authorities claim that a wine is best served from the "respected and romantic container in which it has lived several years of its wonderful life, i.e. the bottle". These persons contend that, provided the bottle has been stood up sufficiently long for the deposit to settle in the punt, the wine can easily be poured into the individual glasses without sacrificing any more than is done in the process of decanting. This procedure would require considerable skill; moreover there are some wines with very loose and difficult deposits, and with these at least decanting is the safer method.

It may be asked: "Why go to all this bother of decanting, why not filter the wine through muslin or some such medium?" The answer is that wine so treated loses its brilliance, and the added exposure to the air in the comparatively slow process of filtration will dissipate the bouquet and most of the ethers of the wine. Unfortunately to-day many people cannot be bothered with decanting, and are more and more demanding wine that is bright to the last drop in the bottle. In order to meet this demand some merchants are prone to perform a large amount of filtering and doctoring, all of which tends to destroy the finer qualities of the wine. A little deposit in a wine is usually a sign of maturity and quality.

8

GLASSES

ONE often wonders who it is that makes the glasses that are offered as wine glasses by the average emporium of to-day, and still more who it is that buys these miserable, poky, thick and ugly little things.

The ideal wine glass should possess four qualities. It should:

Be of plain, clear glass,
Be thin,
Possess a stem,
Be fairly large.

A fifth quality, that of shape, varies somewhat according to the wine to be served and this is a matter of custom, but all wine glasses should be provided with an incurving lip, to assist in the concentration of the bouquet of the wine.

A wine glass should be of plain white glass in order that the eye can play its part in the enjoyment of the wine, the various colours of the different wines being a delight in themselves.

The glass should be thin in order that, if necessary, the wine can be warmed by the heat of the hand, thus bringing out the bouquet.

It should be provided with a stem in order that no unnecessary heat need be applied, besides adding to the beauty of the glass.

It should be fairly large, at least one-third larger than the space necessary for the wine it is to hold, in order to provide room for the concentration of the bouquet.

As for the shape, the saucer-shaped glass which by custom has become associated with the serving of Champagne, is really the worst possible for this type of wine, permitting as it does the rapid dispersion of the effervescence. The ideal glass for Champagne is a tulip-shaped glass with a star cut in the bottom. This star sets up a steady stream of bubbles which make the wine look at its best, whilst the shape keeps the wine lively much longer than the shallow-bowled type could possibly do. The disadvantage of hollow-stemmed

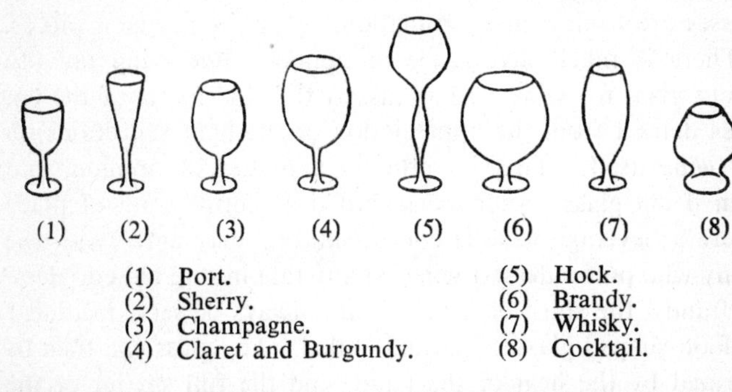

(1) Port.
(2) Sherry.
(3) Champagne.
(4) Claret and Burgundy.
(5) Hock.
(6) Brandy.
(7) Whisky.
(8) Cocktail.

glasses is the difficulty of cleaning them properly. It has even been alleged that the best way of drinking Champagne is out of a beer tankard. With this the writer cannot agree, but then that is perhaps because of a preference even for beer from a glass. When really thirsty one could, presumably, enjoy water out of a jam jar, but that is not the civilised way of serving even that commodity.

Still beverage wines are best served in fairly large, bowl-shaped glasses with an incurved lip. When only partly filled, this type of glass not only allows for the concentration of the bouquet, but also for a slight rocking of the glass to release that bouquet.

Sherry is usually served in long, thin glasses, only partly filled, which again allows the wine to be swirled to release the bouquet.

Glasses for Port generally have an egg-shaped bowl, possessing no incurved lip. This magnificent wine is usually generous in the matter of bouquet, so that the omission of an incurve is perhaps pardonable in this case.

Hock and Moselle, from ancient custom, are usually served in the long typical German glass, but please let it be uncoloured. Formerly nearly all wine glasses were coloured. This was no doubt due to the necessity of hiding the " fliers " so prevalent in the white wines of the past. Coloured wine glasses are to-day an abomination, except as museum pieces.

There is much divergence of opinion concerning the use of cut glass for wine. Many assert that the facets of the cut glass detract from the appreciation of the light reflections on the wine itself. That is certainly a matter of opinion, and even if cut glass should be regarded as entirely out of place where a beverage wine is concerned, one may agree with the many who prefer dessert wines at any rate in rare old cut glass.

Brandy, the spirit of wine, should always be served in large balloon-shaped glasses sparingly filled. The glass can then be warmed by the heat of the hand, and the full savour of the spirit obtained. The heating of the brandy " ballon " by means of a spirit lamp, as is practised in some restaurants, is considered wrong by many connoisseurs. Invariably the glass is made too warm, and the heat of the hand is really quite sufficient to bring out the savour of the spirit, unless of course the glasses have been stored in a refrigerator.

It cannot be over-emphasised that all glasses for wine should be scrupulously clean; moreover the cloth used for this purpose should be exclusively reserved for it. It is very easy for a glass to get a distinct taint by being polished with a cloth which has been used for some other purpose. Neither is it generally appreciated that glasses which have been wrapped in paper should be cleansed and polished before being used. The paper can impart an undesirable taste to the wine. Glasses, too, which have been stored on a deal shelf are apt to get a taint from the wood, which is inimical to wine. In any case it is always a good practice to give all wine glasses a clean and polish before use.

Make sure that the glasses for red wine are brought into the room with the wine, so that they too may take the room temperature.

All this may sound very fussy, but then wine is worth making a fuss about.

9

WINE AND ADDITIVES

THIS subject at once raises the question as to whether the practice of adding a little water to wine is, or is not, a correct one. The answer depends entirely upon the wine in question. Some young beverage wines are definitely improved by the addition of a little water in the glass, as this tends to soften the wine and give it a more mature taste, but only a madman would think of watering down a wine of supreme class.

Most authorities will agreee that Grand Cru wines should be drunk as such, and apart from making sure that they are served at the correct temperature, they should never be adulterated or " improved ". Some ordinaire wines, however, on occasion lend themselves to different forms of presentation, such as in cups, and punches. There are some who enjoy Port with lemonade, and Burgundy with tonic water, and provided the wine is not one of very great elegance there is nothing inherently wrong in such practices, especially when the wine is so mediocre that its consumption in such a form actually adds to the enjoyment of it. The writer is not prepared to extend the same tolerance to " Sangaree ", an American concoction of Port or Sherry with sugar and ice, but again there must be many who will disagree with this point of view.

The vexed question of whether the product of the grape should be " married " to that of grain, is another matter of taste and choice. Certainly vermouth goes well with gin, and ginger wine with whisky, but then neither of the wines mentioned can be called true wines. The addition of brandy to wine in certain circumstances should offer no offence to the most particular, as both are a product of the grape. Some very good drinks can be prepared from wine, and below are given a few reasonable recipes for making use of wine otherwise than as a straight drink—with a word of warning that one should never spoil great wine in the process.

CUPS AND COBBLERS

The former are usually made in a jug from beverage wines, and afford an economical method of providing cooling alcoholic refreshment in hot weather. The latter are made in individual glasses.

Champagne Cup

1 lump of ice, 1 liqueur glass of Apricot Brandy, 1 liqueur glass of Curaçao, 2 liqueur glasses of Brandy, 1 bottle of iced Champagne, 1 bottle of cold soda water. Stir and decorate with fresh fruit in season, add a sprig of mint, borage or sliced cucumber.

Hock Cup

Substitute Hock for Champagne and omit the Apricot Brandy.

Royal Cup

1 bottle of iced Champagne, ¼ bottle of Brandy and nothing else.

Claret Cup

Proceed as for Champagne cup but substitute Claret for Champagne and lemon juice for the Apricot Brandy.

Or alternatively: decant one bottle of Claret into a jug, add one pint of lemonade and decorate with slices of fruit. (Soda water may be used in place of lemonade, but in this case add 1 tablespoonful of sugar.)

Cobblers

These are usually made in the individual glass from dessert wines with shaved ice, and decorated with slices of fruit.

MULLED DRINKS

These are heated drinks with added spices.

Mulled Claret

Bring one bottle of Claret nearly to the boil, add ½ pint of boiling water and enough sugar to sweeten, flavour with sliced orange and six cloves, or with nutmeg and cinnamon.

Mulled Port

Heat the wine gently in a saucepan with a little lemon juice and one or two cloves.

Bishop, Archbishop and Cardinal

Bishop is Port and sugar made hot with a clove-ridden orange added. Archbishop and Cardinal are similar but made with Claret and Hock respectively.

PUNCHES

These may be served either hot or cold.

Cold Champagne Punch

Half fill a cocktail shaker with broken ice, add 1 tablespoonful of sugar syrup, the juice of ½ a lemon, and 1 tablespoonful of Curaçao, well shake and strain, add iced Champagne and decorate with fruit.

Hot Sauternes Punch

Heat the wine with a few slices of orange and a similar portion of lemon, until the surface is covered with small bubbles. Remove and add an infusion of tea leaves in a small muslin bag, leave for five minutes under cover, return to the fire, and add a little blazing Rum, and when burnt off serve at once.

GLOSSARY OF TERMS APPEARING IN THE TEXT

Alcohol	Converted sugar. The potable alcohols are all of the same denomination, i.e. Ethyl alcohol.
Aldehyde	Product of the first oxidation of alcohol, gives character to some wines.
Aperitifs (French)	Appetisers. Drinks taken before a meal to stimulate the appetite.
Ballon (French)	Large balloon shaped glass for service of Brandy, so shaped to conserve the bouquet of the spirit.
Beverage wines	Lightly alcoholic wines suitable for drinking in fairish quantity with main dishes of a meal.
Bin, binning	Rack or recess in which wine bottles are stored in the horizontal position. Act of so placing.
Blending	The mixing together of two or more wines in order to combine the qualities of each in one complete whole.
Bottle	This term usually implies the standard bottle of twenty-six and two-thirds ozs., or six to a gallon.
Bouquet (French)	The perfume of a wine as appreciated by the sense of smell, mainly due to volatile ethers.
British wine	Wine made in Great Britain from imported grape juice which is usually first concentrated by dehydration.
Brown (of wine)	This colour in wine is usually produced by the addition of colour wine or caramel (burnt sugar).
Cane spirit	Spirit made from the distillation of the fermented product of cane sugar or its by-products.
Carbonic acid gas	The gas produced by fermentation, gives characteristic sparkle to Champagne, also used for the "aeration" of Table waters.
Chambrer (French)	Term used of wine which has been brought to the dining room in sufficient time for it to take the temperature of the room before consumption.
Chaptalisation	The practice of the addition of cane or beet sugar to the "must" to increase the ultimate alcoholic strength of the wine.
Château (French)	Castle or country seat. The estate where an individual wine has been grown and produced.
Cochineal	Red colouring matter obtained from an insect and used for colouring liqueurs, food, and also for faking Rosé wines.

Colour wine	Simmered down " must " to which fully fermented wine is added, and used for colouring other wines.
Côte (French)	Literally " Coast " but applied also to hillsides (where better wines can be grown than on the plains).
Cradle	Wicker basket for maintaining the horizontal position of a wine bottle. Main use is for decanting, but some people prefer to serve from them.
Crust	The firm deposit thrown by some wines during maturation in bottle, notably Vintage Port.
Decanting	Transferring wine from a bottle to another container for the purpose of serving, and/or avoiding the deposit or crust.
Dégorgement (French)	The process of removing the deposit from the bottles of sparkling wines, prior to their shipment.
Dehydration	The removal of water from a substance. With grape juice it is done in a vacuum, thus avoiding cooked taste.
Dessert wines	Wines suitable for use with or after the dessert, mostly of the fortified and/or sweet type.
Dry (of wine)	Not sweet. Appreciated by some connoisseurs, but average taste is for semi-dry.
Duty	Tax payable on alcoholic liquors. With wine is based on degrees of alcohol regardless of quality.
Eau de Vie de Marc (French)	A form of Brandy made from the " murk " left over from ordinary wine making. Is quite palatable if given time to mature.
Empire wines	Term applied to wines made within the British Empire, many of which are of fine quality.
Ethers	Light volatile compounds giving bouquet to the fine wines.
Fermentation	Conversion of sugar into alcohol, is brought about by an enzyme contained in the yeast germ.
Fino	Term applied to Sherry which has developed "flor" (which see). Such wines are fine and delicate.
Flagon	Term applied to a bottle of the capacity of one imperial quart. Some are squat, some round, and some oval.
Fliers	Light, floating material having appearance of sand, sometimes occurring in white wine. Has no bad effect and usually disappears with an increase in the temperature.
Flor	White organic growth produced on the surface of some maturing Sherries, converting some of the alcohol into aldehyde and giving character to the wine.

Fortified wines — Those to which an addition of spirit (usually Brandy) has been made. Examples Port and Sherry.

Frappé (French) — Term used of a wine which has been sufficiently iced to improve the flavour, usually only white wines so treated.

Full bodied — Applied to wine which has a distinct body (this may be alcoholic or merely aromatic) as opposed to a thin wine.

Half bottle — Term applied to a bottle of half the capacity of the standard bottle, i.e. twelve to the gallon.

Improved wines — A somewhat misleading term for wines which have had an addition of sugar to the "must". These wines are never as good as those made from grapes containing sufficient of their own sugar.

Liqueur — Sweetened and flavoured alcohol in which all the ingredients are intimately mixed. The term is often wrongly applied to old Brandy, and other *unsweetened* spirits.

Made wine — Term applied to sparkling wines which usually have additions *made* to them.

Magnum — A bottle of the capacity of two ordinary bottles, and mostly used in connection with Champagne.

Marc (French) — The refuse left over from the making of wine, which by further pressings and addition of water and sugar, produces an inferior type of wine.

Mature (of wine) — One which has delevoped its full character and finesse usually only with bottle age.

Medicated wines — Those to which an addition of medicaments has been made, and for which additional tonic qualities are therefore claimed.

Millésime (French) — The date of the vintage.

Must — The name given to the juice of freshly gathered grapes before it has fermented into wine.

Mutage (French) — The practice of the artificial checking of the fermentation of a wine.

Natural wines — Those to which no addition has been made, but which have been allowed to ferment naturally.

Old (of wines) — Many wines are undrinkable until they have attained a certain bottle age, but some are best drunk young. An old wine is not necessarily therefore a best wine.

Ordinaire (French) — Term applied to wholesome ordinary wines which have no pretension of posing as fine wines.

Plastering — Term used for the practice of adding Calcium sulphate to a wine in order to increase the acidity. Was originally done with Plaster of Paris, hence name.

Platrage (French) — The French term for the above. The practice is rarely resorted to nowadays.

Punt — The pushed-in end of continental bottles. It is done to add strength to the bottle.

Racking — The process of drawing wine off its lees into fresh casks.

Red (of wine) — Red wine is obtained from black grapes by allowing the wine to ferment on the husks. The pigment which is contained only in the skins is soluble in the alcohol produced by the fermentation.

Red Biddy — Some atrocious concoctions once offered as British wine but mainly consisting of industrial alcohol.

Rosé (French) — Pink wine obtained from black grapes, the skins of which are left in the " must " only long enough to give a pink tinge. Some Rosé wines are made from mixing black and white grapes, or blending red and white wine.

Sack — Old English name for Canary and Sherry wines. The word to-day is used to denote a dry Sherry.

Schloss (German) — Equivalent of French Château. The estate on which an individual wine has been produced.

Sommelier (French) — Wine butler or waiter. A Guild of British Sommeliers has recently been formed, all good luck to them!

Sparkling (of wine) — Truly named sparkling wines are produced by allowing the secondary fermentation of the wine to take place in the bottle, thus retaining the natural gas of the action.

Sulphuring — The treatment of casks with sulphur to sterilise them against microbean pests. A general and reasonable practice. Also refers to the addition of Sulphurous acid to white wine to prevent further fermentation, which is a somewhat dubious practice.

Sweetening wine — Wine produced by the addition to unfermented " must " of fully fermented wine. It is used for giving sweetness to other wines lacking a sufficiency.

Table wines — Synonymous with Beverage wines (which see).

Tannin — A product of Tannic acid found in most wines, but in a greater proportion in red wines. Too much tannin gives the wine an astringency.

Tartaric acid	An acid normally present in wine, much of which is deposited in the form of tartrates in the lees. When a wine lacks sufficient acidity Tartaric acid is now more commonly used than Calcium sulphate to increase the acid content.
Tawny (of wine)	A rust-like tinge assumed by wine which has been maturing in cask for a number of years. Such wines are usually very mellow.
Tonic wines	Another name for medicated wines (which see).
Trocken-beerenauslese (German)	Dry grape selection. Applied to wine made from selected "sleepy" grapes. These contain proportionately a greater amount of sugar and produce luscious wine.
Vermouth	Wine to which has been added a maceration of herbs, the principal of which is wormwood (German "Wermuth"), hence name. It makes a splendid aperitif.
Vigneron (French)	The vineyard owner, and usually the maker of his own wine.
Vignoble (French)	Term for a vineyard or collection of vineyards.
Vin, Vins (French)	Wine, wines.
Vin de Marc (French)	Inferior wine made by the addition of water and sugar to the last pressing of the refuse of wine making.
Vin de Presse (French)	Inferior wine made from the first pressing of the marc, usually without addition.
Vinification	The making of wine.
Weepers	Bottles which show a slight leakage at the cork. They should be re-corked or consumed before deterioration ensues.
Wein (German)	Wine.
White (of wine)	So called white wine is never truly white, but ranges from pale amber to deep golden and sometimes with a green tinge. White wine can be made from either white or black grapes, in the case of the latter, by the removal of the skins from the "must".
Wood	Term used to denote casks, e.g. wine from the wood, as opposed to bottled wine.
Yeast	A living organism containing an enzyme capable of converting sugar to alcohol. The bloom on the outside of a grape is a form of yeast.
Young (of wine)	Without age. Some wines are best drunk young, but nearly all wines require about two years in cask to develop before bottling.

CANISIUS COLLEGE LIBRARY
TP548 .C3 c. 1
Wine lore;a critical
3 5084 00141 4807

BUFFALO, N. Y.